PERIPLUS NATURE GUIDES

TROPICAL REEF FISHES

of Malaysia & Singapore

Text by Gerald R. Allen, Ph.D.

Photography by
Roger Steene, Gerald R. Allen,
Rudie Kuiter, Mark Strickland,
Burt Jones, Maurine Shimlock,
Fiona Nichols, Charles Anderson,
Ashley Boyd, and Matthew Hedrick

PERIPLUS

Published by Periplus Editions (HK) Ltd.

Printed in Singapore.
ISBN: 962-593-867-2

Publisher: Eric M. Oey
Design: Peter Ivey
Editor: Michael Stachels

Distributors
Indonesia
PT Java Books Indonesia
Jl. Kelapa Gading Kirana
Blok A14 No. 17, Jakarta 14240

Japan / Korea
Tuttle Publishing
RK Bldg, 2nd Floor 2-13-10 Shimo-Meguro
Meguro-ku Tokyo 153 0064

North America
Tuttle Publishing
Distribution Center, Airport Industrial Park,
364 Innovation Drive,
North Clarendon, VT 05759-9436

Southeast Asia
Berkeley Books Pte Ltd
5 Little Road, #08-01
Singapore 536983

Introduction

Fishes are by far the most abundant group of vertebrates—approximately 24,000 species inhabit fresh and marine waters. They are also the oldest backboned animals, having evolved in ancient seas nearly 500 million years ago. An incredible variety of habitats are populated by fishes—virtually every conceivable aquatic environment, from deep ocean trenches to high alpine streams. The group is so diverse it is difficult to define them, but most breathe by means of gills, have a protective layer of scales, and propel themselves through water (a medium that is 800 times denser than air) by means of fins. However, there are numerous exceptions—eels, for example, usually lack scales and have either much reduced fins or none at all.

Warm, clear seas of the Indo-Pacific, the vast region stretching between East Africa and the islands of Polynesia, have nurtured the development of nature's richest realm—the living coral reef. This region, centred on the Indonesian-Philippine Archipelago, is the world's most extraordinary biological province. Nowhere else can one find such a wealth of colourful and diverse marine life. More than half of the world's total fishes are found in this region. They range in size from the gargantuan, 12-metre-long Whale shark to diminutive gobies that are smaller than one's fingernail.

Except for a relatively small number of locally or regionally restricted species, known as endemics, most fishes in the Indo-Pacific have broad distributions—in many cases ranging all the way from Africa to Polynesia. Their broad dispersal is the result of the pelagic larval stage common to most reef fishes, in which the tiny young are propelled through surface waters by winds, waves and currents. The end result is a closely interrelated community of fishes inhabiting the length and breadth of the Indo-Pacific region. This is clearly an advantage for anyone wishing to learn the fishes of different localities within this vast area. Nearly all families, most genera and many species will be the same regardless of whether you are at Tahiti, Indonesia or the Maldive Islands.

The tremendous abundance of fishes seen during a single scuba dive or snorkeling session may seem staggering. Indeed, in some areas one can find as many as 300 species inhabiting only one or two hectares of reef. But there is no need to despair. This Periplus Nature Guide is an excellent introduction to the reef's most commonly encountered species. The entries are grouped according to family, and arranged in conventional taxonomic order. An index which includes both common and scientific names can be found at the end of the book. Fish watching is the aquatic counterpart of bird and butterfly watching. Almost anyone can enjoy this enriching hobby. The only essential equipment is a mask and snorkel, although of swim fins are also a good investment. Every fish that you encounter has an interesting story to tell about its unique habits and special way of life.

Leopard Shark

Stegostoma fasciatum

Family:
Stegostomatidae

The Leopard shark is distinguished by a whisker or "barbel" at each corner of the mouth, prominent ridges on the side of the body and a huge tail, which makes up about one-half of its total length. Adults, which grow to more than 300 cm, have a distinctive pattern of leopard-like spots. Another common name for this species is Zebra shark, based on the juvenile pattern—primarily black with vertical white bands. Of all the sharks in the tropical Indo-Pacific region it is among the easiest to identify due to its colour, shape and habit of resting on the bottom. It feeds mainly on gastropod and bivalve molluscs, but crustaceans (crabs and prawns) and small fishes are also eaten. There is very little information about its behaviour, other than its habit of lying on the bottom for long periods. Females are known to deposit several large (approximately 8 x 17 cm), blackish egg cases. There are no reports of human attacks by this species. It pays little attention to divers or flees at their approach.

MARK STRICKLAND

Blacktip Reef Shark

Carcharhinus melanopterus

Family:
Carcharhinidae

This is one of the most commonly seen sharks in the Indo-Pacific region. It prefers shallow water close to shore, often on reef flats as shallow as 30 cm. Maturity occurs at a size of about 100 cm and the maximum length is about 170 cm. The young, which are born alive, measure between 33 and 52 cm. The Blacktip is an active, strong-swimming shark that occurs singly or in small groups. The diet consists mainly of small fish, cephalopods and shrimps. While not considered a dangerous shark, it has attacked humans. Most attacks appear to be cases of "mistaken identity"—instinctively homing in on the wader's splashes and mistaking the disturbance for struggling fish. The species is commonly seen in public aquaria.

In the 1960s, the author sent the first live shipment of young Blacktips to the Steinhart Aquarium in California. The sharks were captured by hand at low tide on the reef flat at Enewetak Atoll in the central Pacific.

RUDIE KUITER

Silvertip Shark

Carcharhinus albimarginatus

Family:
Charcharhinidae

This sleek predator is common in clear water, particularly on steep slopes, below depths of 20–30 metres. The geographic range extends from East Africa and the Red Sea to the Pacific coast of Central America. It is a dangerous species that is known to attack humans. It has the habit of passing uncomfortably close to divers should they enter its territory. Its normal food consists of a variety of fishes, including wahoo, eagle rays, wrasses and tunas. It will also consume octopuses and squids.

This shark should not be confused with the Reef whitetip, a harmless, relatively sluggish species that is often seen in shallow water. Both sharks have similar white markings on the dorsal and caudal fin, but the Whitetip is more slender and lacks white on the pectoral fin tips. The maximum size of the Silvertip is about 200 cm. The young, which measure between 63 and 68 cm, are born alive. Each litter contains 5 or 6 babies, but there may be as many as 11.

ASHLEY BOYD

Scalloped Hammerhead Shark

Sphyrna lewini

Family: Sphyrnidae

The odd head shape typical of this family of sharks has been the subject of considerable speculation. Scientists believe it serves a twofold purpose of increasing manoeuvrability and enhancing sensory capabilities. The uniquely flattened head acts as a bowplane, allowing it to move swiftly through the water. The expanded surface area along the front of the "hammer" is crammed with special sensory cells for detecting pressure changes and electromagnetic fields, not unlike the sensor plate of a metal detector. In addition, the widely-spaced eyes may enhance their binocular vision.

The family contains nine species, of which the Scalloped hammerhead is one of the most common and widely distributed. It occurs in all tropical and warm-temperate seas. They sometimes congregate over sea mounts or around offshore islands, forming schools of hundreds of individuals. This shark is potentially dangerous, but attacks are rare. Maximum size is about 400 cm.

JONES/SHIMLOCK

Manta Ray

Manta birostris

Family: Mobulidae

The distinctive Manta rays are easily recognised by the pair of large protruding flaps in front of the mouth, the lateral eyes, large wing-like appendages (actually modified pectoral fins), lack of a tail spine (some may have a rudimentary spine) and the tiny dorsal fin at the base of the tail. The head flaps are used to swoosh planktonic food into the mouth. It is ironic that such a huge animal feeds on tiny zooplankton. The largest mantas are reported to grow to a width of nearly 7 m and weigh more than 1,300 kg, making them one of the largest of all fishes. The family occurs in all warm seas—about 10 species are known. Large mantas are frequently sighted from boats, sometimes far out to sea. They are also regularly encountered by divers in the vicinity of coral reefs. One of the best areas to view them is around Sangalaki Island, off the northeastern coast of Kalimantan (Indonesian Borneo). Here they can be seen almost every day of the year, often performing spectacular leaps above the surface.

JONES/SHIMLOCK

Ribbon Eel

Rhinomuraena quaesita

Family: Muraenidae

The bright-coloured Ribbon eel is aptly named. Although the head is roughly cylindrical, its body is thin and ribbon-like. Unlike most morays belonging to the same family, it lives in sandy burrows. It is usually seen protruding its head and up to about one-third of the body length outside the burrow. Aside from coloration and shape, the most distinguishing feature is the enormously expanded nostrils, which form a membranous scoop-like structure. If threatened, for example when closely approached by a diver, the eel swiftly retreats into its burrow, waiting several minutes before emerging.

Juveniles and small adults are mainly black with a yellow dorsal fin. Males become blue on the body and have a characteristic yellow snout. Adult females are entirely yellow except for white fin margins and a black anal fin. The species is widely distributed in the Indo-West Pacific region, ranging from East Africa to the Tuamotus and northwards to Japan. Maximum length is at least 130 cm.

MARK STRICKLAND

Giant Moray

Gymnothorax javanicus

Family: Muraenidae

There are dozens of moray eel species on tropical coral reefs, but most are shy and seldom seen. They inhabit the endless cracks and fissures that riddle the reef's surface. The Giant moray is a notable exception that is often sighted by divers and has a particularly vicious appearance. Growing to a length of at least 2.2 metres and 30 kg weight, it is the largest moray eel living in the vast Indo-Pacific region. Like most morays, its jaws are equipped with numerous sharp fangs, which are normally used for capturing fishes or crustaceans. However, they can inflict nasty wounds on careless divers. For this reason it is not advisable to blindly probe deep crevices with your arms while diving, possibly in search of shells or lobsters. Nor is it advisable to spear large eels. They can easily spin off a spear and may vent their anger by biting savagely. In contrast, unprovoked specimens are usually docile and will allow divers to photograph them at close range or even feed and pet them.

ROGER STEENE

Striped Catfish

Plotosus lineatus

Family: Plotosidae

Catfishes are usually thought of as being freshwater inhabitants, but are prominent in marine waters of Southeast Asia. Although most are confined to estuaries and turbid coastal waters, the Striped catfish is commonly encountered on coral reefs. Juveniles are most seen. They typically form aggregations which contain up to several hundred fish massed tightly together, with individuals actually in contact with one another. The aggregation takes on the appearance of a much larger creature or even inanimate objects, reducing the chances of predation. Large catfishes have few enemies due to their very venomous fin spines. Extreme care should be exercised when handling them as the puncture wounds are excruciatingly painful.

There is scant reproductive information on the Striped catfish. Males build nests under rocks or large pieces of debris and guard the eggs. The species ranges from the Red Sea to Samoa. Maximum size is 32 cm.

JONES/SHIMLOCK

Spotfin Squirrelfish

Sargocentron cornutum

Family:
Holocentridae

Although very abundant on coral reefs, squirrelfishes are seldom noticed by snorkellers. They remain hidden deep in the shadows of caves and crevices during daylight hours. Shortly after sunset they begin to emerge for nocturnal feeding. Because most of the reef's fish occupants are active during the day, many invertebrates, particularly crustaceans and echinoderms, have evolved a strategy to avoid them by coming out to feed at night. Squirrelfishes have adapted night-time feeding to take advantage of this behaviour. They mainly consume crustaceans, particularly small crabs and shrimps.

Squirrelfishes are easily recognised by their red coloration, coarse scales and large eyes. Another remarkable feature is their ability to produce clearly audible "clicking" sounds, believed to function as a form of communication between members of the school. Most species, such as the Spotfin squirrelfish, are less than 25 cm when fully grown, but the largest attains 45 cm.

MARK STRICKLAND

Trumpetfish

Aulostomus chinensis

Family: Aulostomidae

The bizarre Trumpetfish is found throughout the Indo-Pacific region, from Africa to the Americas. Its peculiarities include an elongate body, tubular snout, and a small barbel or chin "whisker". The colour pattern is largely greenish or brownish with diffuse pale stripes and bars, but it can quickly change its colours to blend with the surroundings. Occasional individuals are bright yellow. It occurs solitarily in most reef habitats, including inshore shallows and outer reefs to depths of over 100 m. This slow-swimming predator relies partly on stealth and camouflage to sneak up on unsuspecting victims, usually small fishes, which are quickly sucked into the mouth with a vacuum-cleaner action. It is sometimes seen hovering vertically with its head aiming downwards. This position gives it the appearance of an innocuous bit of stick or weed, and is perfect for launching a rapid, downward attack. The trumpetfish family contains only three species. Their maximum length is about 80 cm.

GERALD ALLEN

Smallscale Scorpionfish

Scorpaenopsis oxycephalus

Family:
Scorpaenidae

Scorpionfishes are masters of disguise. Their excellent camouflage blends exceptionally well with the surroundings. They are "lay and wait" predators, which can remain motionless for hours, patiently waiting for unsuspecting prey to pass within close range of their cavernous mouth. Their usual food consists of small fishes and crustaceans, which are swallowed whole in a single, lightning-quick gulp. The 30-cm-long Smallscale scorpionfish is one of the larger coral reef-dwelling members of the family. It lives in a variety of habitats, but is most frequently seen in clear water on outer reef slopes. The colour is variable, depending on depth and surroundings. Fishes from deeper water (below about 15 m) tend to be reddish, whereas those from shallow depths are often brown or greenish. The filamentous skin flaps on the head and body help to enhance its disguise, appearing like a growth of stubbly sea weed. The family gets its name from the venomous dorsal, anal and pelvic fin spines.

JONES/SHIMLOCK

Leaf Scorpionfish

Taenianotus triacanthus

Family: Scorpaenidae

The wafer-thin Leaf scorpionfish occurs on coral reefs across the entire width of the Indo-Pacific region, from Africa to the Galapagos. Like most scorpionfishes it is a clever camouflage artist. Its shape, colouration, and motion effectively mimic non-movable objects such as sponge and seaweed, luring its victims into a false sense of security. It feeds on small fishes and crustaceans. It is so confident in its camouflage that is shows little resistance and is easily scooped with a small hand net. The species does well in an aquarium, but must be offered a diet of live food.

When encountered on the reef, one must be exceptionally lucky to see it. It assumes the colour of its surroundings—shades of red, yellow, white, tan and black are commonly seen. Typically the fish sits in one position, propped by its large, flexible pectoral fins, and rocks gently from side to side, as though swaying to the rhythm of the currents.

GERALD ALLEN

Red Firefish or Lionfish

Pterois volitans

Family: Scorpaenidae

There are approximately 12 species of firefishes and lionfishes occurring on coral reefs of the Indo-Pacific region. They are distinguished by the over-sized pectoral fins. In the genus *Pterois* the tips of the pectoral rays protrude as separate filaments, whereas in *Dendrochirus* the rays have a solid membrane between them, giving a "webbed" appearance. The widely distributed Red firefish is among the largest species (to about 38 cm) commonly seen. It has particularly long, feather-like pectoral-fin rays. When fully fanned and thrust forward these fins are useful in cornering nocturnal prey, usually crabs and shrimps, occasionally fishes. Daylight hours are spent resting under ledges, in caves or among wreckage—either singly or in aggregations.

The venomous dorsal, anal and pelvic fin spines are used as a defensive weapon. Their wounds are particularly painful. The recommended first aid treatment is to soak the wound in very hot water.

MATHEW HEDRICK

Flame Anthias

Pseudanthias ignitus

Family: Serranidae
Subfamily: Anthiinae

The exquisite Flame anthias is found on coral reefs of the eastern Indian Ocean, from the Maldive Islands to the Andaman Sea. An almost identical species, the Redfin anthias (*Pseudanthias dispar*), occurs in Indonesia and throughout much of the western Pacific. However, it differs in lacking the broad red stripe on the upper and lower edges of the tail. Both species have similar behaviour and live in identical habitat situations. They occur in aggregations, most frequently in clear waters of outer reef slopes and passes in depths ranging from about 3 to 15 m. Zooplankton is the main dietary item and the group swims up to several metres above the bottom while feeding. When threatened by passing divers or predators the anthias hastily retreat to the safety of rocky crevices. Like most anthias they have a harem-type social structure, with each male controlling a group of females. When courting the male colours are greatly intensified and the bright red dorsal fin is fully erected.

MARK STRICKLAND

Square-blotched Anthias

Pseudanthias pleurotaenia

Family: Serranidae
Subfamily: Anthiinae

The grouper family (Serranidae) contains a diverse assemblage of more than 400 reef fishes occurring worldwide. Most of us think of groupers as large, chunky fishes that live close to the reef's surface. But the more than 100 members of the subfamily Anthiinae, commonly called anthias, are quite different in appearance. They are delicate, bright-coloured fishes, which swim in aggregations—often numbering in the hundreds—high above the bottom. They are usually common in clear water, where currents are periodically strong. They depend on the current-borne supply of zooplankton for nourishment. Most species, including the Square-blotched anthias, have a fascinating social structure. Each male maintains a "harem" of several females. If the male dies or is eaten by a predator, the dominant (frequently the largest) female changes to the male sex over a period of several days, and takes charge of the harem. Maximum size of the Square-blotched anthias is 20 cm.

JONES/SHIMLOCK

Coral Grouper

Cephalopholis miniata

Family: Serranidae

Groupers and their relatives in the family Serranidae are a dominant element of the fish community on all coral reefs, particularly in the Indo-Pacific region. The larger species are important table fish at many localities and the small schooling members, for instance the numerous anthias (or Fairy basslets) no doubt play an important role in the reef's food chain. Members of the genus *Cephalopholis* are small to medium-sized groupers (also know as cods or rockcods in Australia) that occur in a variety of coral reef habitats. The Coral grouper, with its bright red coat studded with blue spots, is among the most colourful species. It grows to a reported length of 41 cm and is most often encountered in clear water of outer reefs to depths of at least 150 m. Like most of the larger groupers it feeds mainly on small fishes, supplemented by crustaceans. Feeding occurs mainly during the early morning and midafternoon. The favourite food appears to be small, schooling anthias.

FIONA NICHOLS

Giant Grouper

Epinephelus lanceolatus

Family: Serranidae

The Giant grouper holds the distinction of being the largest of all bony fishes occuring on coral reefs. There are reports of particularly huge individuals weighing as much as 400 kg and measuring nearly 3 m. These monsters are usually just curious towards divers. They either approach at close range for a brief moment, or may spend several minutes following them from a safe distance. Although the details are vague and none are fully documented, there are a few reports of fatal attacks on humans. One precaution that divers must take is to never try and hand-feed large individuals. At least one person learned this lesson the hard way on Australia's Great Barrier Reef. A young man offered a struggling fish he had just speared. The Giant grouper's response was lightning quick—the fish was literally inhaled, along with the man's arm. Luckily he managed to jerk his arm out of the mouth, but in the process it was severely lacerated by the numerous rows of small, sharp teeth.

ROGER STEENE

Coronation Grouper

Variola louti

Family: Serranidae

The Coronation grouper frequents clear water areas of the tropical Indian and Pacific oceans. It is distinguished from most relatives by its striking colour pattern and characteristic yellow-edged, lunar-shaped tail. A nearly identical species, *Variola albimarginata,* is sometimes seen in the same areas, but it has a white edge on the tail instead of a yellow edge. The habitat usually consists of outer reefs from shallow depths down to at least 240 m where it is caught by handline fishermen. The Coronation grouper feeds mainly on coral reef fishes, but also consumes crabs and other crustaceans. The flesh is excellent eating and much in demand. However, at a few isolated locations, where the reef has been disturbed, large fish have been implicated in cases of human ciguatera poisoning. This potentially fatal toxin is actually produced by a type of algal scum (dinoflagellate) that lives on dead coral and seaweed. It is transmitted through the food chain, from plant-eating fishes to predators.

ROGER STEENE

Banggai Cardinalfish

Pterapogon kauderni

Family: Apogonidae

Although first collected in 1920 by a Dutch physician, this strikingly handsome fish was all but forgotten until recently. It was rediscovered at Banggai Island, off the east coast of central Sulawesi, by journalist Kal Muller, who photographed it underwater. This prompted the author to visit this locality in order to collect and photograph this unusual fish for the Western Australian Museum. It lives in shallow water next to shore among clumps of seagrass. Groups of two to about 60 fish were seen associated with long-spined *Diadema* sea urchins. Small juveniles seldom stray from the urchin's spines and adults retreat among them if frightened. Cardinalfishes are well known for the male's habit of incubating a mass of eggs in its mouth, but the Banggai cardinalfish carries this care one step further. It shelters a brood of 10–15 babies in its mouth, the only marine fish (out of approximately 14,000 species) known to exhibit this unusual behaviour. This species grows to about 6 cm.

GERALD ALLEN

Bigeye Trevally

Caranx sexfasciatus

Family: Carangidae

Trevallies or jacks are sleek, swift fish predators occurring in all tropical and subtropical seas. Most are highly regarded table fishes and are therefore targeted by sport anglers and commercial fishers. The Bigeye trevally grows to 78 cm and is commonly encountered on the edge of coral reefs, usually in schools that may contain hundreds of individuals. Squadrons of these fast-moving fishes, their silver bodies reflecting wave-dappled sunlight, form an impressive sight. Young fish are often found in brackish estuaries or even in freshwater. Apparently these nursery areas provide an abundance of food and there are fewer predators compared to the reef habitat. Subadults eventually migrate to clear offshore waters. Most feeding occurs at night or during twilight. During the day they are often seen in nearly stationary milling schools. Most family members are fish predators, but a few species eat mainly molluscs and crustaceans, or planktonic invertebrates.

RUDIE KUITER

Blue and Gold Fusilier

Caesio teres

Family: Caesionidae

Fusiliers are an integral part of the Indo-Pacific fish community. They are often one of the first fishes noticed after slipping below the surface with scuba gear, especially on outer reef slopes or in passes washed by strong currents. Mixed shoals, containing hundreds of individuals belonging to several species, constantly patrol the reef's periphery. They sometimes exhibit "swarming" behaviour, completely surrounding a diver, who is temporarily obscured from view by the mass of swirling fishes. Their schooling behaviour is designed to confuse predators. The probability of an individual member of a large school being attacked and eaten is very small. When faced with the confusing mass of numbers, a potential predator finds it difficult to visually "lock" onto a single target. The family contains about 20 species. Most are predominantly blue, but have variations with regards to the shape and extent of yellow markings on the body, as well as markings on the tail. This species grows to 30 cm.

GERALD ALLEN

Oriental Sweetlips

Plectorhinchus orientalis

Family: Haemulidae

Sweetlips in the genus *Plectorhinchus* have a snapper-like appearance with relatively large fleshy lips. They are generally solitary in habit, but sometimes form large daytime resting aggregations. At night they actively feed on a wide variety of bottom-living invertebrates, especially crustaceans. Members of the genus are noted for their bold colour patterns and the Oriental sweetlips is no exception. Young sweetlips are coloured very differently from the adults and it is sometimes difficult to link the two stages without detailed study. However, the juvenile of the Oriental sweetlips is well known. It is primarily dark brown with a white snout and breast, 2–3 white saddles along the back, and a pair of diagonal white bands across the tail. Small juveniles of all species swim with an exaggerated side-to-side swimming motion. They are highly prized by marine aquarists. The Oriental sweetlips ranges from East Africa to Samoa and northwards to the Ryukyu Islands. It grows to 86 cm.

MARK STRICKLAND

Butterflyfishes

Family:
Chaetodontidae

Butterflyfishes have long been a favourite of underwater photographers and aquarists, displaying a remarkable array of colour patterns. Most exhibit shades of yellow, orange, or white with prominent black or brown spots, stripes, or bands, or a combination of these features.

The family is well represented in tropical seas—about 120 species have been described to date. Most belong to the genus *Chaetodon*, which are generally ovate or rounded in profile, with a relatively thin body. All butterflyfishes have sharp spines on the front half of the dorsal fin, which are used as a defensive weapon. In most cases the spines, although prominent, adhere to the general body profile. But in the bannerfishes (genus *Heniochus*), those on the anterior part of the fin form a long, graceful pennant-like filament.

Most species live on sections of the reef where there is prolific coral growth. This is not merely a coincidence as the diet of many butterflyfishes consists wholly or at least partially of living coral polyps. Other species eat a combination of small bottom-living invertebrates and algae, but use the coral growth for shelter. The social behaviour of butterflyfishes has been the subject of several scientific studies. Butterflyfishes are generally "home-ranging"—they are restricted to individual reefs or a limited section of more extensive reef complexes. During the day they search for food within the confines of the range, retiring among coral crevices when darkness descends. Some fish return to the identical resting place every evening. Studies indicate that some species, such as the Saddled butterflyfish shown on the opposite page, form lifetime pairs and rarely lose sight of one another. Other species, such as the Racoon butterflyfish, also form pairs, but may occur alone or in groups. A few species are invariably seen in large aggregations.

ROGER STEENE

Raccoon Butterflyfish
Chaetodon lunula

ROGER STEENE

Bennett's Butterflyfish
Chaetodon bennetti

ROGER STEENE

Pacific Double-saddle Butterflyfish
Chaetodon ulietensis

ROGER STEENE

Ornate Butterflyfish
Chaetodon ornatissimus

ROGER STEENE

Saddled Butterflyfish
Chaetodon ephippium

Teira Batfish

Platax teira

Family: Ephippidae

The graceful batfishes are a favourite of underwater photographers. Five species occur in the Indo-Pacific area, all belonging to the genus *Platax*. The handsome juveniles make excellent aquarium pets. They become tame very quickly and will accept feedings by hand. The young have highly exaggerated dorsal, anal, and pelvic fins. For example, an 8-cm-long Teira batfish may measure over 25 cm from dorsal fin tip to anal fin tip. As the fish grows older the fins become proportionally smaller, until the shape is approximately round. Young fish are usually seen hovering under coral heads or in the shadows of boat moorings and wharves. At least two species employ clever disguises in their youthful stage to avoid predation. The Round-faced batfish (*Platax orbicularis*) lies on its side and drifts back and forth with the waves, appearing very much like a water-logged leaf. The tiny young of the Pinnate batfish (*Platax pinnatus*) swim on their side with a strange undulating motion—mimicking a toxic polyclad flatworm.

JONES/SHIMLOCK

Longfin Bannerfish

Heniochus acuminatus

Family:
Chaetodontidae

The Longfin bannerfish is recognised by its bold black and white bands and the very elongate dorsal fin, which forms a graceful, backward-flowing filament. A very similar species, the Schooling bannerfish (*Heniochus diphreutes*), sometimes occurs in the same reef environment, but the two species are easily differentiated on the basis of behaviour. The Longfin is encountered singly, in pairs, or small groups, and usually swims close to the bottom. In contrast, the Schooling bannerfish forms large aggregations that swim high above the bottom. Despite their behavioural differences both species exhibit similar dietary preferences, feeding largely on a combination of zooplankton and small bottom-living invertebrates such as worms and shrimps. The bannerfish genus *Heniochus* includes a total of eight species which inhabit coral reefs of the Indo-West Pacific. The Longfin and its Schooling cousin are among the most widespread species, occurring from East Africa to Polynesia.

MARK STRICKLAND

Anemonefishes

Family:
Pomacentridae

Subfamily:
Amphiprioninae

The partnership between certain damselfishes belonging to the family Pomacentridae and relatively large tropical sea anemones is one of the reef's most fascinating sights. British naturalist, Dr. Cuthbert Collingwood, was the first European to witness and describe it. This was more than 125 years ago on the shores of Borneo. Anemonefishes have been thrust into the limelight ever since. Not only have they been the subject of numerous scientific studies, but they are now heralded as the world's most popular marine aquarium fishes.

Twenty-eight different species are known. All but one, the Spinecheek anemonefish (*Premnas biaculeatus*), belong to the genus *Amphiprion*. Most species have a colour pattern consisting of an orange, red or black background and one to three vertical white bands. They inhabit the vast Indo-Pacific region, extending from the shores of East Africa and the Red Sea eastward to Polynesia. The largest number of species occur in the area that includes Indonesia, Philippines and New Guinea.

They are never found without a host anemone, which offers a safe refuge among its tentacles. The tentacles are covered with microscopic stinging cells, which keeps most fish intruders at bay. However, a special chemical substance in the anemonefish's skin mucus prevents the stinging cells from firing. Ten species of anemones are found together with anemonefishes. Only the widely distributed Clark's anemonefish (*Amphiprion clarkii*) cannot tolerate every type of anemone. Most are found with only three or four anemone species, and several are confined to just a single species. The fishes lay several hundred eggs at the base of their host, in a position where the veil of protective tentacles continually sweeps over them. Closely guarded by the male parent, the eggs hatch after 6–7 days. The larvae are free-swimming for about 1–2 weeks, then they must find an anemone or perish.

Tomato Anemonefish
Amphiprion frenatus

Pink Anemonefish
Amphiprion perideraion

Clark's Anemonefish
Amphiprion clarkii

Spinecheek Anemonefish
Premnas biaculeatus

False Clown Anemonefish
Amphiprion ocellaris

Angelfishes

Family:
Pomacanthidae

The colourful angelfishes are among the most conspicuous members of the reef community. They are readily distinguished from the equally colourful and closely related butterflyfishes (family Chaetodontidae) by the presence of an enlarged, backward projecting spine on the cheek. About 85 species inhabit tropical seas, but the majority occur in the Indian and West-central Pacific oceans. Their maximum total length ranges from about 7 to 50 cm.

Spawning occurs at dusk and usually involves a single pair, although individual males may mate successively with several different females. Males set up territories by driving away other male competitors. They then swim up off the bottom and await the arrival of one or more females. When a prospective mate approaches, the male exhibits a courtship display that may include fin erection, rapid back and forth swimming and body "quivering". Eventually the pair spiral slowly towards the surface, suddenly shed eggs and sperm at the apex of the ascent, then swim back to the bottom. Hatching of the tiny (less than 1 mm) eggs occurs in 15–20 hours.

Angelfishes offer a dazzling array of patterns—sparking a great deal of scientific controversy about their possible purpose. Many theories have been proposed, but none have been proved with any certainty. Large angelfishes are famous for their dramatically different juvenile patterns, which gradually change as the fish grows older. According to one theory, the striking juvenile livery is actually a type of camouflage, serving to break up the outline of the fish so it effectively blends with the high contrast pattern of bright sunlit patches and shadows that characterise the reef environment. Others maintain that the pattern may warn predators that its sharp spines are an unpalatable mouthful. Bright adult patterns probably help individuals of a particular species to recognise one another for reproductive purposes.

MARK STRICKLAND

Emperor Angelfish
Pomacanthus imperator

RUDIE KUITER

Yellowmask Angelfish
Pomacanthus xanthometopon

ROGER STEENE

Blue-girdled Angelfish
Pomacanthus navarchus

R.C. ANDERSON

Regal Angelfish
Pygoplites diacanthus

MARK STRICKLAND

Blue-ringed Angelfish
Pomacanthus annularis

Indo-Pacific Sergeant

Abudefduf vaigiensis

Family:
Pomacentridae

The common name of this species is based on its broad geographic distribution—from the Red Sea and East African coast to southeastern Polynesia and north to Japan. Along with the Sergeant major (*Abudefduf saxatilis*) from the tropical Atlantic and the Panamanian sergeant (*Abudefduf troschellii*) from the eastern Pacific, it forms a trio of nearly indistinguishable species. They are mainly separable on the basis of subtle colour pattern differences. The Indo-Pacific sergeant usually forms aggregations, sometimes containing hundreds of individuals which swarm over the bottom or swim high above it in search of zooplankton. It is seen in a variety of reef environments—frequently on the upper edge of outer slopes or in a more sheltered situation close to shore. Prior to spawning the male prepares a nest by clearing algae and debris from a bare patch of hard bottom. The nest measures up to 30–40 cm across and may contain as many as 25,000 eggs. These hatch after 5–7 days.

GERALD ALLEN

Blue-green Chromis

Chromis viridis

Family:
Pomacentridae

The Blue-green chromis is abundant across the vast Indo-Pacific region from Africa to Polynesia. It occurs in aggregations associated with branching corals, usually in the genus *Acropora*. Groups may contain several hundred individuals that feed on zooplankton up to several metres above the bottom. When disturbed—for example, if approached by a diver or predatory fish—the school quickly retreats in unison among the coral branches. When the coast is clear they reappear, first forming a blue "halo" a short distance above the coral, then gradually spreading out to resume feeding.

Prior to spawning a single male attracts as many as 20 females to the nest site with a courtship dance consisting of rapid up and down swimming. Up to several thousand eggs are eventually laid, which are guarded by the male for 2–3 days. After hatching the larvae rise to the surface and drift with the currents for 18–24 days. The maximum size is 9 cm.

GERALD ALLEN

Blue Devil

Chrysiptera cyanea

Family:
Pomacentridae

This striking neon-blue damselfish is common on coral reefs of the Western Pacific from Australia northwards to Japan and eastward to the Mariana and Caroline Islands. Mature males generally have bright orange tails, except in some parts of Indonesia. Females have clear or bluish tails and a black spot at the base of the hindmost dorsal-fin rays. The habitat consists of lagoons and protected inshore reefs in knee-depth shallows down to about 10 m. Eggs are laid in rocky crevices after the male lures a mate to his nest with a flurry of rapid chasing, colour pattern change and fin erection. The male chases the female away after spawning and meticulously cares for the developing eggs. This involves chasing away egg thieves, such as wrasses, and frequently swimming back and forth over the nest, presumably to keep the eggs free of debris and possibly to aerate them. Hatching occurs in 3–4 days. The tiny transparent larvae are then free swimming, for 2–3 weeks. Maximum size is about 8.5 cm.

ROGER STEENE

Neon Damsel

Pomacentrus coelestis

Family:
Pomacentridae

Like glittering jewels, huge schools of Neon damsels are a common sight on coral reefs of Southeast Asia. The species ranges widely from Sri Lanka to the central Pacific. The favoured habitat consists of outer reefs in clear water, frequently among coral rubble in areas exposed to slight wave action or strong currents. Depth range extends from about 1 to 12 m. The species has several look-alike relatives: the nearly identical Caerulean damsel (*P. caeruleus*) occurs in the western Indian Ocean; the Goldbelly damsel (*P. auriventris*) from the Malay-Indonesian Archipelago has more yellow on the body and fins; Allen's damsel (*P. alleni*) from the Andaman Sea has a black streak on the lower edge of the tail; and the Similar damsel (*P. similis*), also from the Andaman Sea, has darker dorsal and anal fins. All of these species exhibit similar spawning habits. Eggs are laid on the underside of rocks and guarded for several days until hatching. Maximum size is 9 cm.

ROGER STEENE

Lemon Damsel

Pomacentrus moluccensis

Family:
Pomacentridae

Damselfishes are one of the most conspicuous members of the coral reef fish community. No other family can boast such large numbers. They literally swarm over the reef during daylight hours. About 150 species occur in Southeast Asia. The Lemon damsel is one of the most abundant species in this region. It occurs on coastal, lagoon and outer reefs, in rich areas of live coral, forming aggregations that are closely associated with individual coral formations. The usual depth range is between 1 to 14 m. At most localities the fish is brilliant yellow, but individuals from the Fiji Islands are mainly purple with a yellow tail. This sort of geographic colour variation, although not usually so extreme, is common in many damselfishes. The Lemon damsel feeds on a combination of zooplankton, algae and small bottom-living invertebrates. When spawning each female lays about 1,000 eggs, which are guarded for five days until hatching by the male. Maximum length is 7.5 cm.

RUDIE KUITER

Humbug Dascyllus

Dascyllus aruanus

Family:
Pomacentridae

The damselfish family contains 330 species in tropical and warm temperate seas. Many, such as the Humbug dascyllus, have very precise requirements as far as living conditions are concerned. It is always associated with coral heads (usually *Acropora* or *Pocillopora*) that have a tree-like form, allowing the fish to retreat deep within the branches. Humbugs live only where the coral heads are interspersed with sandy patches, usually in protected lagoons or sheltered bays, only occasionally on outer slopes.

Just prior to spawning the male selects a nest site at the dead base of its home coral head and nips away the fine covering of filamentous algae. It then engages in a jerky display of up-and-down swimming, which attracts females to the nests. Each male may mate with several females at the same nest, but usually only one spawning occurs each day. The male chases away its partner after the eggs are deposited, then meticulously cares for them.

ROGER STEENE

Three-spot Dascyllus

Dascyllus trimaculatus

Family:
Pomacentridae

Also known as the Dominofish, this species is easily recognised by its overall black colouration and small white spot on the back. Juveniles are more intensely black and have a larger white spot as well as an additional white spot on the forehead. They make excellent pets and are popular in the marine aquarium trade. The species is extensively distributed, ranging from the Red Sea and East Africa to Polynesia, and from northern Australia to Japan. It occurs in a variety of rocky and coral reef habitats, from shallow waters to at least 55 m depth.

Courtship and nest preparation are similar to those of other damselfishes. Up to 25,000 eggs are laid on a hard, rocky surface. Males care for the eggs, which hatch in three days. Juveniles are associated with large sea anemones or branching coral heads, upon which they rely for shelter. Those living with anemones are apparently protected from its sting by the same chemical mechanism used by anemonefishes (page 30). Maximum size is 13 cm.

RUDIE KUITER

Giant Wrasse

Cheilinus undulatus

Family: Labridae

Wrasses are the second largest family of reef fishes—only the goby family has more species. The Giant wrasse is the largest member of this group, which contains an estimated 500 species. It grows to a length of at least 230 cm and weight of 190 kg. In spite of its huge bulk it is a shy fish that is difficult to closely approach. Although Giant wrasse is certainly an appropriate name, it is also known as the Humphead wrasse or Napoleon fish. The only fish it is likely to be confused with is the Bumphead parrotfish (*Bolbometopon muricatum*), which reaches 130 cm. However, the parrotfish has a highly distinctive head profile, which is nearly square. The Giant wrasse is usually seen singly in clear waters of outer reef slopes in 10–100 m depth. It feeds on a wide variety of molluscs, fishes, sea urchins, crustaceans and other invertebrates. The notorious coral-destroying Crown-of-thorns starfish is also occasionally consumed. The Giant wrasse ranges widely in the Indo-Pacific region.

GERALD ALLEN

Yellowtail Coris

Coris gaimard

Family: Labridae

The Yellowtail coris frequents sand and rubble patches intermingled with coral where it feeds on small invertebrates. Juveniles are brilliant red with four white saddles along the top of the head and back. This pattern gradually disappears with increased growth and is replaced by the adult colours shown here. Like most wrasses, the Yellowtail begins its adult life as a female and can later transform to the male sex—at which time a different, usually gaudier, colour pattern is assumed. In some species there are both mature males and females in the initial adult phase—these tend to spawn in aggregations. The brightly coloured terminal male, however, only spawns with a single partner. Some species, such as the Yellowtail coris, appear to engage only in pair spawning. Eggs and sperm are released at the apex of a rapid dash towards the surface. The eggs are buoyant and float to the surface. The subsequent larval stage is pelagic for several weeks. Maximum length is 40 cm.

GERALD ALLEN

Cleaner Wrasse

Labroides dimidiatus

Family: Labridae

Cleaner wrasses are important to the health of local fish communities throughout the Indo-Pacific region. They feed on external parasites, often tiny crustaceans known as copepods, from the body, mouth and gill chamber of other fishes. Solitary fish or small groups, often composed of a single male and several females, establish cleaning "stations" at more or less permanent locations around the reef. Their characteristic colour pattern and peculiar bobbing "dance" advertise their presence to a long, and varied list of customers. There is such a demand for their services that individual fish will visit the station several times a day, and may even form queues to wait their turn. The Cleaner wrasses often service huge predatory fishes that, if given the chance, would normally eat most species of wrasses. Yet the Cleaner is allowed to freely enter the mouth while the predator yawns widely. The five species of Cleaner wrasses (all in the genus *Labroides*) range in size from about 8 to 12 cm.

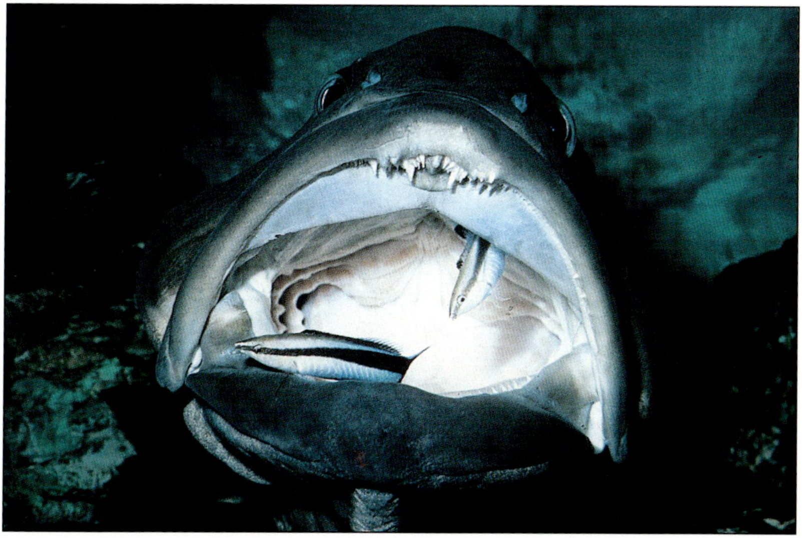

RUDIE KUITER

Bumphead Parrotfish

Bolbometopon muricatum

Family: Scaridae

A school of these giants is one of the reef's most spectacular sights—an underwater version of a herd of grazing bison. They travel in small groups, usually containing about 5–20 individuals. In spite of their considerable bulk (to 120 cm and 50 kg) these fish are very shy and usually swim away when divers approach. They feed on live coal and also filamentous algae that form a fine layer on hard surfaces. When feeding they make loud scraping noises. As in most parrotfishes, the teeth are fused into beak-like plates—an ideal tool for removing coral and algae. A considerable amount of rock fragments is also swallowed and is ground together with the algae by special teeth at the back of the throat—a process that aids the digestion of plant material. The rocky bits are pulverized to sand and go through the digestive tract, eventually being passed out of the body with the faeces. Studies indicate that parrotfishes are a major producer of sediment in tropical seas. The Bumphead ranges from East Africa to Samoa.

JONES/SHIMLOCK

Blue-barred Parrotfish

Scarus ghobban

Family: Scaridae

Parrotfishes are characterized by sex reversal and frequently undergo a series of radical colour pattern changes between the juvenile and adult stages. Adults of most species exhibit two different patterns, depending on whether they are in the "initial" or "terminal" phase. Initial phase fish are either male or female and generally are less colourful than the gaudy terminal phase (seen here), which is invariably male. Initial phase females can change to the male sex and take on the brighter colours of the terminal phase. Colour changes within each species have caused an unbelievable amount of confusion among fish scientists. In some cases, the juvenile, initial phase, and terminal phase of the same species were given separate scientific names. Poor communication between scientists in the 18th and 19th centuries made things even worse—in many cases scientists from different countries assigned several names to the same fish. The Blue-barred parrotfish was named on 22 separate occasions! It grows to 75 cm.

GERALD ALLEN

Chevron Barracuda

Sphyraena qenie

Family: Sphyraenidae

Barracudas are well-known fishes occurring worldwide in tropical and warm temperate seas. They have a long, slender body with pointed snout, and the large mouth is equipped with an awesome array of unequal-sized sharp teeth. The Chevron barracuda is one of the larger species, growing to about 1 m in length. It ranges widely in the tropical Indo-Pacific and is usually encountered in large milling schools in clear water. Most barracudas are harmless, but in the West Indies the Great barracuda (*Sphyraena barracuda*) is feared even more than sharks. More than 30 human attacks have been recorded. In some cases the victims were wearing a wristwatch or other type of reflective jewellery, while dangling hands or feet in the water from a boat or jetty. Barracudas are instinctive predators that can strike with lightning speed. Most likely the jewellery was mistaken for a small, struggling fish. Few, if any attacks have involved scuba divers, and attacks are rare in our region.

GERALD ALLEN

Jawfishes

Opistognathus sp.

Family:
Opistognathidae

Behaviourally, the jawfishes are among the reef's most interesting inhabitants. They construct elaborate pebble and shell-lined burrows on sand and rubble bottoms adjacent to reefs. The burrow consists of a vertical shaft and a terminal chamber. The fish are often seen with only the head or eyes peering out from the entrance. When feeding they pop staight up, exposing their full body length for a few seconds before retreating into the burrow. Most species appear to feed chiefly on zooplankton, but they are also known to make short excursions in search of benthic invertebrates.

Males lure gravid females with spectacular courtship displays involving colour changes and fin erection. When successful the male enters the burrow first and is followed by the female, who lays her eggs in the terminal chamber. The egg mass is tended by the male, who periodically picks it up and "juggles" it in its mouth. Most species are under 15 cm in length.

JONES/SHIMLOCK

Fire Dartfish

Nemateleotris magnifica

Family:
Microdesmidae

This elegant species is a common inhabitant of rubble channels and sandy ledges on outer reef slopes. The depth range extends from about 6 to over 50 m. It usually occurs in mated pairs and the partners appear to communicate with one another by rapidly flicking the banner-like dorsal fin. Typically the pair hovers a short distance above the bottom, feeding in the current on planktonic animals. When frightened they quickly dart into the burrow head first, emerging when the coast is clear. The author once did an experiment to establish the nature of the burrow. Liquid resin was poured into a burrow and allowed to set before retracting it. The burrow had a sinuous shape, was about 35 cm long and ended in a small chamber next to solid rock. There is little information about the reproductive habits, but presumably eggs are laid in the burrow and tended by one or both parents. The species ranges from East Africa to the Hawaiian Islands. Maximum size is 7 cm.

MARK STRICKLAND

Blueband Goby

Valenciennea strigata

Family: Gobiidae

Gobies are by far the largest family of fishes in the world with an estimated 2,000 species. They are incredibly diverse with regards to appearance, behaviour and habitat. Although the majority of species are tropical marine inhabitants, they are also well represented in cooler seas, as well as fresh waters. To the casual coral reef visitor, they are not particularly conspicuous—primarily because many are very small and have cryptic habits. Most of the reef-dwelling gobies are less than 20 cm in length, and there are a huge number that mature well under 3 cm. A few species are fully mature at 8–10 mm! The Blueband goby and its relatives in the genus *Valenciennea* are among the larger species. They grow to a length of about 10–18 cm. Pairs are usually seen on rubble bottoms down to about 20 m depth. They excavate burrows under rock slabs by removing mouthfuls of sand. Eggs are laid in the burrow and guarded by the parents until hatching. The Blueband goby feeds mainly on small invertebrates.

ROGER STEENE

Moorish Idol

Zanclus cornutus

Family: Zanclidae

The boldly-patterned Moorish idol is arguably the most readily recognised of all coral reef fishes. It is the sole representative of its family and one of the widest ranging coral fishes in the Indo-Pacific region, occurring from the Persian Gulf, Red Sea and East Africa to the shores of Central America. It is most common in shallow water between 5–20 m. Solitary fish or small groups are most often encountered, but occasional large schools with up to a hundred or more individuals may occur. Freshly spawned eggs are buoyant and drift with the currents. The duration of the larval stage is unknown, but judging from the geographic distribution of adults, it probably extends for at least 6–8 weeks. The largely transparent larvae are readily attracted to a light suspended just below the surface. They grow to a remarkably large size (about 8 cm) before settling to the bottom and assuming the typical colour pattern. Sponges form a significant portion of the diet. Maximum length is 16 cm.

MARK STRICKLAND

Palette Surgeonfish

Paracanthurus hepatus

Family: Acanthuridae

The incredible design on the coat of the Palette surgeonfish is its most distinctive feature. Indonesians refer to it as *Angka enam* ("number six"), because the black marking on the side roughly resembles the numeral six. The species ranges widely in the Indo-Pacific region, from Africa eastward to Samoa and the Gilbert Islands (Kiribati). It is generally found in clear water of outer reefs or channels where there are strong currents. Adults are almost impossible to approach closely and juveniles hide among the branches of live coral. It is very difficult to photograph. When feeding they rise well off the bottom, facing into the current, in order to capture zooplankton. Like most surgeonfishes it has a single collapsible scalpel-like spine on each side of the tail base, which can be erected at right angles to the body if threatened. Each spine folds into a shallow groove when not in use. This is the only species in the genus *Paracanthurus*. It grows to a maximum length of about 30 cm.

ROGER STEENE

Striped Surgeonfish

Acanthurus lineatus

Family: Acanthuridae

This very beautiful surgeonfish is common on coral reefs throughout the Indo-Pacific, from Africa eastward to the Marquesas and Tuamotu Islands. It is absent from the Red Sea, where it is replaced by a very similar species, *Acanthurus sohal.* The habitat consists of shallow reefs exposed to wave action. This species has two peculiarities that differ from most other surgeonfishes. Firstly, the collapsible scalpel-like spine on each side of the tail base is venomous and capable of causing very painful wounds if the fish is carelessly handled. Secondly, the species is strongly territorial, aggressively chasing away intruders that enter their domain. The territory of each adult occupies about 6–8 sq m. Attacks are mainly against other algal-feeding fishes such as surgeonfishes, parrotfishes, and triggerfishes—but are often directed towards other Lined surgeons. This behaviour ensures an adequate supply of seaweed-covered turf, which is its sole food source. Maximum size is 38 cm.

GERALD ALLEN

Yellowkeel Unicornfish

Naso lituratus

Family: Acanthuridae

The Yellowkeel unicornfish is one of the most distinctive members of the surgeonfish family. It has an unmistakable yellow-edged black mask extending from the eyes to the snout, black dorsal fin, and a pair of bright orange spines just in front of the tail. Unlike most other surgeonfishes, which have a single collapsible spine on each side of the tail base, those of the Yellowkeel and other unicornfishes (genus *Naso*) are paired and immovable. The spines function as a defensive weapon. The Yellowkeel is generally sighted alone or in small groups, but occasional large aggregations are seen. It is often shy and difficult to approach at close range when snorkelling or scuba diving. Individuals are generally "home-ranging", each occupying large sections of reef, where they forage for leafy brown sea weeds such as *Sargassum*. Its extensive distribution ranges from the Red Sea and East Africa to remote Clipperton Island in the eastern Pacific. Maximum size of the Yellowkeel is 45 cm.

MARK STRICKLAND

Spotted Unicornfish

Naso brevirostris

Family: Acanthuridae

The 17 species of unicornfishes in the genus *Naso* are members of the surgeonfish family. They are primarily distinguished from other surgeons by a pair of scalpel-like blades on each side of the tail base and, as the common name suggests, several species have a unicorn-like horn above the snout. Most species frequent clear waters of outer reefs, particularly adjacent to steep slopes. The Spotted unicornfish is easily recognised by the very long slender horn of adults and pattern of dark spots and broken lines on the side. As in other species possessing a nasal horn, this feature is lacking in juveniles, but gradually develops with increased growth. Unicornfishes pick zooplankton from passing currents, high above the bottom, in contrast to their surgeonfish cousins, which mainly eat filamentous sea weed. Group spawning is common and males often exhibit greatly enhanced courtship colouration. Maximum size of this species is about 50 cm.

ROGER STEENE

Foxface

Siganus vulpinus

Family: Siganidae

The Foxface is one of the most colourful members of the family Siganidae, commonly known as rabbitfishes because of their rabbit-like snout. In Australia they are called Spinefeet due to the unusual structure of the pelvic fins (located under the breast). In most fishes this paired fin is either spineless or has a single spine on its outer edge—but the Foxface and its relatives have an outer and inner spine with three soft rays between them on each side. These spines, and also those of the dorsal and anal fins are venomous and capable of producing very painful wounds, although generally not as serious as those inflicted by scorpionfishes. The family contains 28 species, which are confined to the Indo-Pacific region. The Foxface ranges from western Sumatra eastward to the Caroline and Marshall Islands. It is usually seen in rich coral areas. Young fish occur in schools, but form permanent pairs at a length of about 10 cm. Maximum length is about 24 cm.

RUDIE KUITER

Clown Triggerfish

Balistoides conspicillum

Family: Balistidae

The triggerfish family contains about 40 species, which are distributed in tropical seas. All have a similar, rugby-ball shape, but most are easily separated by their distinctive colour patterns. The Clown trigger is easily the most spectacular with its garish pattern of large white polka dots contrasting strongly with the surrounding jet-black colouration. The species is understandably a favourite of marine aquarists. Several decades ago, when it first appeared in pet shops, the price tag was over US$300 per fish. Nowadays it is more common, but still fetches at least $50. The habitat consists of clear waters of outer reef slopes at depths between about 5 and 75 m. Juveniles are very secretive, mainly confining themselves to caves below 20 m depth on steep drop offs. It is usually seen alone, although courting pairs are occasionally encountered. The three dorsal spines, just behind the head, are seldom erected. Maximum length of the Clown triggerfish is about 50 cm.

MARK STRICKLAND

Orange-lined Triggerfish

Balistapus undulatus

Family: Balistidae

The Orange-lined triggerfish is widely distributed, from East Africa to the central Pacific. The habitat consists of coral-rich areas of lagoons and seaward reefs at depths between 2 and 50 m. Individuals are solitary and appear to be territorial, but the behaviour has not been studied in detail. Although information for this species is lacking, it probably spawns in similar fashion to other triggerfishes: a shallow crater-shaped nest is excavated on sand/rubble bottoms and the eggs are guarded by the female. In some of the larger triggerfishes (especially the Titan trigger), aggressive tendencies are greatly enhanced at this time and attacks on divers are common. Triggers have powerful jaws with chisel-like teeth and can deliver a painful bite. Like other members of the family, the Orange-lined triggerfish seeks shelter in coral crevices when threatened or when retiring for the night. This species feeds on algae, coral, sea urchins, crabs, molluscs, starfish, worms and sponges. Maximum size is 30 cm.

ROGER STEENE

Coral Filefish

Oxymonacanthus longirostris

Family:
Monacanthidae

The 10-cm-long Coral filefish ranges from East Africa to Samoa, and from Australia north to Japan. It is easily distinguished from other members of the family by its elongate snout and bright pattern of orange dots. It feeds on live coral polyps and is therefore restricted to areas of abundant coral growth in depths between 1 and 30 m. Pairs are commonly encountered among branching or "tabletop" corals. Filefishes obtain their name from the rough texture of the skin—when dried it was formerly used as sandpaper by South Sea islanders. In Australia these fishes are known as leatherjackets. The family, which is very closely related to triggerfishes, contains about 85 species, which are found in tropical and temperate seas. Australia has nearly 60 species, far more than any other region—but most are confined to cooler seas around the southern half of the island continent. They are an important commercial fish in both Australia and Japan.

RUDIE HUITER

Yellow Boxfish

Ostracion cubicus

Family: Ostraciidae

Boxfishes are bizarre creatures that have the body encased in bony carapace. They are slow swimmers, propelling themselves with a sculling movement of the dorsal and anal fins. Rather than using speed to flee from enemies they rely on their coat of armour, and some species produce a skin toxin, which is released when the fish is stressed. If a boxfish is placed in a bucket or small aquarium with other fishes and then harassed, the toxin will quickly kill all the occupants and may even prove fatal to the boxfish if the concentration is high enough. Boxfishes feed on a wide variety of bottom living animals —especially stationary forms such as sponges, sea squirts, and soft coals. Algae is also consumed. The Yellow boxfish is the most commonly encountered member of the family in the Indo-Pacific region. Juveniles are bright yellow with black dots. With increased growth the fish gradually become brown and the spots may disappear entirely. Maximum size is 45 cm.

ROGER STEENE

Sharpnose Puffer

Canthigaster valentini

Family:
Tetraodontidae

About 25 species of Sharpnose puffers inhabit tropical seas of the Indo-Pacific region. They were formerly considered a separate group, but are now included in the same family with other puffers. Aside from their small size, they differ from most other marine puffers with regard to head shape (especially the elongate snout). They can also erect low skin ridges—one running down the middle of the back, and another along the belly. Most of the species inhabit shallow water in the vicinity of coral reefs, sand flats, rubble bottoms, wreckage and wharf pilings. A wide variety of food items are consumed including algae, coral polyps, shellfish, crabs, sponges, worms and sea squirts. Like other puffers, the sharpnose group is capable of causing a violent form of fish poisoning if the flesh or internal organs are eaten by humans. For added protection, sharpnose puffers also produce a skin toxin. The Sharpnose puffer is mimicked by an almost identical filefish (*Paraluteres prionurus*).

RUDIE KUITER

Black-spotted Puffer

Arothron nigropunctatus

Family:
Tetraodontidae

The comical-looking pufferfishes, although never abundant, are frequently noticed inhabitants of coral reefs. Instead of relying on speed to flee from enemies, they have evolved other escape methods. First and foremost is their ability to swallow water (or air when out of water), causing the body to inflate to several times its normal size into a spherical ball. In addition, a potent poison is produced in their tissues, particularly the liver and ovaries. If humans eat the flesh it may result in serious illness and even death. Ironically, puffers are considered a delicacy in Japan. The flesh is detoxified and carefully prepared for eating by specially licensed chefs. Still, it produces a mildly intoxicating affect when consumed. The Black-spotted puffer ranges from East Africa to the central Pacific. It feeds mainly on live corals, but also consumes sponges, tunicates and algae. Maximum length is about 25 cm. Normally the fish is blue-grey with black spots, but some individuals are partly or almost solid yellow.

ROGER STEENE

Freckled Porcupinefish

Diodon holocanthus

Family: Diodontidae

Porcupinefishes are close relatives of puffers, and like their cousins can swallow air or water to greatly inflate the body. It's not difficult to guess how they received their common name—they are covered with spiny projections. Just like its mammalian namesake these are erected when threatened and used as a defensive weapon. However, most potential predators realise the folly of trying to make a meal of this fish and give it a wide berth. The only real threat is from sharks, which occasionally devour them. About 20 species of porcupinefishes are known. They are mainly found on tropical reefs. The shape and arrangement of their spines is a useful feature for separating the different species. In some, the spines are relatively long and movable, but in others, they form short, thorn-like projections. Their strong, fused teeth are ideally suited for crushing shells of sea urchins, crabs and shellfish, which are the main dietary items. The Freckled porcupinefish is found worldwide. It attains lengths of 29 cm.

RUDIE KUITER

Index

Abudefduf vaigiensis 34
Acanthurus lineatus 52
Amphiprion clarkii 30, 31
Amphiprion frenatus 31
Amphiprion ocellaris 31
Amphiprion perideraion 31
anemonefishes 30, 31
angelfishes 32, 33
Arothron nigropunctatus 61
Aulostomus chinensis 13
Balistapus undulatus 57
Balistoides conspicillum 56
Banggai cardinalfish 22
Bennett's butterflyfish 27
Bigeye trevally 23
Black-spotted puffer 61
Blacktip reef shark 5
Blue and gold fusilier 24
Blue devil 36
Blue-barred parrotfish 45
Blue-girdled angelfish 33
Blue-green chromis 35
Blue-ringed angelfish 33
Blueband goby 49
Bolbometopon muricatum 44
Bumphead parrotfish 44
butterflyfishes 26, 27
Caesio teres 24
Canthigaster valentini 60
Caranx sexfasciatus 23
Carcharhinus albimarginatus 6
Carcharhinus melanopterus 5
Cephalopholis miniata 19
Chaetodon bennetti 27
Chaetodon ephippium 26, 27
Chaetodon lunula 26, 27
Chaetodon ornatissimus 27
Chaetodon ulietensis 27
Cheilinus undulatus 41
Chevron barracuda 46
Chromis viridis 35
Chrysiptera cyanea 36
Clark's anemonefish 30, 31
Cleaner wrasse 43
Clown triggerfish 56
Coral filefish .58
Coral grouper 19
Coris gaimard 42
Coronation grouper 21
Dascyllus aruanus 39
Dascyllus trimaculatus 40
Diodon holocanthus 62
Emperor angelfish 33
Epinephelus lanceolatus 20
False clown anemonefish 31
Fire dartfish .48
Flame anthias 17
Foxface 55
Freckled porcupinefish 62
Giant grouper 20
Giant moray .10
Giant wrasse 41
Gymnothorax javanicus 10
Heniochus acuminatus 29
Humbug dascyllus 39
Indo-Pacific sergeant 34
Jawfish 47
Labroides dimidatus 43
Leaf scorpionfish 15
Lemon damsel 38
Leopard shark 4
Longfin bannerfish 29
Manta birostris 8
Manta ray 8
Moorish idol 50
Naso brevirostris 54
Naso lituratus 53
Nemateleotris magnifica 48

Neon damsel 37
Opistognathus sp. 47
Orange-lined triggerfish 57
Oriental sweetlips 25
Ornate butterflyfish 27
Ostracion cubicus 59
Oxymonacanthus longirostris 58
Pacific double-saddle butterflyfish . . .27
Palette surgeonfish 51
Paracanthurus hepatus 51
Pink anemonefish 31
Platax teira 28
Plectorhinchus orientalis 25
Plotosus lineatus 11
Pomacanthus annularis 33
Pomacanthus imperator 33
Pomacanthus navarchus 33
Pomacanthus xanthometopon 33
Pomacentrus coelestis 37
Pomacentrus moluccensis 38
Premnas biaculeatus 30, 31
Pseudanthias ignitus 17
Pseudanthias pleurotaenia 18
Pterapogon kauderni 22
Pterois volitans 16
Pygoplites diacanthus 33
Raccoon butterflyfish 26, 27
Red firefish or lionfish 16
Regal angelfish 33
Rhinomuraena quaesita 9
Ribbon eel 9
Saddled butterflyfish 26, 27
Sargocentron cornutum 12
Scalloped hammerhead shark 7
Scarus ghobban 45
Scorpaenopsis oxycephalus 14
Sharpnose puffer 60
Siganus vulpinus 55
Silvertip shark 6
Smallscale scorpionfish 14
Sphyraena barracuda 46
Sphyrna lewini 7
Spinecheek anemonefish 30, 31
Spotfin squirrelfish 12
Spotted unicornfish 54
Square-blotched anthias 18
Stegostoma fasciatum 4
Striped catfish 11
Striped surgeonfish 52
Taenianotus triacanthus 15
Teira batfish .28
Three-spot dascyllus 40
Tomato anemonefish 31
Trumpetfish 13
Valenciennea strigata 49
Variola louti 21
Yellow boxfish 59
Yellowkeel unicornfish 53
Yellowmask angelfish 33
Yellowtail coris 42
Zanclus cornutus 50